Pillbug

Stephanie St. Pierre

Heinemann Library
Chicago, Illinois

Published by Heinemann Library,
an imprint of Reed Educational & Professional Publishing,
Chicago, Illinois
Customer Service 888-454-2279

Visit our website at www.heinemannlibrary.com

Designed by Wilkinson Design
Illustration by David Westerfield
Printed and bound in Hong Kong

06 05 04 03 02
10 9 8 7 6 5 4 3 2 1
Library of Congress Cataloging-in-Publication Data

St. Pierre, Stephanie
    Pillbug / Stephanie St. Pierre.
        p. cm. -- (Bug books)
    Includes bibliographical references (p.).
    ISBN 1-58810-174-6 (lib. bdg.)   ISBN 1-58810-927-5 (pbk. bdg.)
    1. Armadillidium vulgare--Juvenile literature. [1. Wood lice
    (Crustaceans)]   I. Title. II. Series.
    QL444.M34 S72 2001
    595.3'72--dc21
00-012400

Acknowledgments

The author and publishers are grateful to the following for permission to reproduce copyright material:
Cover: Donald Specker/Animals Animals
pp. 4, 7, 13 Donald Specker/Animals Animals; p. 5 Robert Dunne/Bruce Coleman, Inc.; p. 6 Ken Brate/Photo Researchers, Inc.; pp. 8, 17, 20-22, 26, 27, 29a, 29b Dwight Kuhn; p. 9 Kevin Schafer/Peter Arnold, Inc.; p. 10 Dwight Kuhn/Bruce Coleman, Inc; p. 11 Biophoto Associates/Photo Researchers, Inc.; p. 12 Clyde H. Smith/Peter Arnold, Inc.; p. 14 G. Buttner/Naturbild/OKAPIA/Photo Researchers, Inc.; pp. 15, 24, 25 Corbis; pp. 16, 23 James P. Rowan; p. 18 Holt Studios International/Photo Researchers; p. 19 Ken Brate/Photo Researchers, Inc.; p. 28 Robert Jackman/Oxford Scientific Films.

Special thanks to James Rowan for his help in the preparation of this book.

Every effort has been made to contact copyright holders of any material reproduced in this book. Any omissions will be rectified in subsequent printings if notice is given to the publisher.

Some words are shown in bold, **like this.**
You can find out what they mean by looking in the glossary.

Contents

What Are Pillbugs?

Pillbugs are not **insects.** They are **crustaceans.** Crustaceans are animals with hard shells. Their shells have many pieces. Crustaceans are close relatives of insects.

The hard pieces of the pillbug's body are its **exoskeleton.** An exoskeleton is a skeleton on the outside of an animal's body. It protects the soft parts of the animal's body.

What Do Pillbugs Look Like?

Pillbugs are small gray bugs. When they are rolled into a ball they are about the size of a pea. They have seven pairs of legs and a rounded shell. Their bellies are flat. They have short **antennae.**

It's hard to see a pillbug's belly. When they are bothered, pillbugs roll up into little balls. Pillbugs are sometimes called roly-polys. They are called pillbugs because they look like pills.

How Are Pillbugs Born?

Pillbug eggs hatch in a pouch in the mother's belly. There may be as many as two hundred eggs in the pouch. They **hatch** after three to seven weeks.

A group of pillbugs born together is called a **brood.** Most **female** pillbugs have two broods each year. They have one brood in the spring, and one brood in the summer. The broods hatch in warm, **damp** places like these woods.

How Do Pillbugs Grow?

The mother pillbug carries her babies in the pouch for over a month. The babies are white. Their bodies are soft. They look like tiny grown-up pillbugs.

Pillbug babies' shells harden and darken as they grow. When they get bigger, they find homes of their own. They shed their shells many times.

How Do Pillbugs Change?

When pillbugs are born they have only six pairs of legs. When they shed their shells for the first time they grow their seventh pair of legs.

Pillbugs cannot move around in the cold. They only shed their shells in summer. In the winter they **hibernate** until it gets warm again in the spring.

What Do Pillbugs Eat?

This pile of grass clippings makes a perfect meal for pillbugs. Pillbugs also eat dead leaves and old fruit. They will even eat rotting logs.

Sometimes pillbugs will eat live plants. Pillbugs have not hurt this plant. But they can hurt plants if they eat away their roots and new growth.

Where Do Pillbugs Live?

Pillbugs do not live in water like most of their relatives. But they do need to stay **moist.** If a pillbug gets too dry it will die.

Pillbugs choose **damp** places to live. They live under rocks, in dead logs, and in other dark, cool places. They usually die indoors unless it is very damp.

What Do Pillbugs Do?

Pillbugs **recycle.** By eating dead plants pillbugs help to make the soil richer. This helps new plants to grow.

In winter, the water that pillbugs need to live is frozen. Pillbugs do not do much in the winter. They go under rocks and logs and stay still until the weather warms up.

How Do Pillbugs Move?

Pillbugs are crawlers. They move very slowly and it takes them a long time to get anywhere. They cannot run away from danger. They roll up instead.

During her lifetime a **female** pillbug might have babies six times. There can be 200 babies in each **brood.** A pillbug can have over 1,000 babies in just 3 years.

Which Animals Attack Pillbugs?

Pillbugs have many enemies. **Shrews,** toads, frogs, and lizards eat pillbugs. Small owls and some foxes eat them too.

These are not the only **predators** that eat pillbugs. Spiders, centipedes, and some beetles eat pillbugs. Pillbugs will eat other pillbugs that are **molting.**

How Are Pillbugs Special?

Pillbugs are the only bugs that can roll up when they are bothered. You can pick them up and see how they roll into balls. Be careful not to hurt them.

You can keep pillbugs as pets. Keep
them in a jar with holes poked in the lid.
Put some **damp** dirt in the jar. Feed the
pillbugs leaves and potato peelings.
Spray the jar with water every week.

Thinking about Pillbugs

Which of these animals is related to
the pillbug? Do you remember what the
pillbug does when it is scared?

This boy wants to keep some pillbugs as pets. What will he feed them? Should he make sure their new home is damp or dry? Should it be warm or cold?

Bug Map

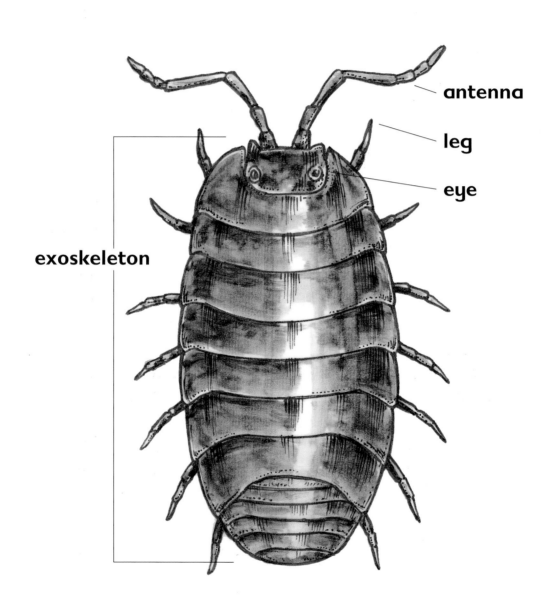

antenna

leg

eye

exoskeleton

Glossary

antenna (more than one are called antennae) long, thin tube that sticks out from the head of an insect. Antennae can be used to smell, feel, hear, or sense direction.

brood group of babies that hatch at the same time

crustacean relative of insects that has a tough shell, including pillbugs, sowbugs, shrimp, lobsters, and crabs

damp a little bit wet

exoskeleton hard shell on the outside of an animal's body

female girl or woman

hatch to be born out of an egg

hibernate to sleep or not move much during the winter months

insect small animal with six legs

moist slightly wet

molting shedding the old, outer layer of skin that has been outgrown

nocturnal animal that is active at night, and sleeps during the day

predator animal that hunts and eats other animals

recycle to take waste and make it into something useful

shrew animal that is related to a mole and eats insects

More Books to Read

Himmelman, John. *A Pill Bug's Life*. Danbury, Conn.: Children's Press, 2000.

Souza, Dorothy M. *Insects in the Garden*. Minneapolis, Minn.: Lerner Publishing Group, 1991.

Index